Looking at History   R J Unstead

Book Two

The Middle Ages

Adam and Charles Black   London

Acknowledgements

Aerofilms Ltd   10
City of Bayeux   6a, b & c, 7a, b & c
Trustees of the British Museum   1, 3, 4, 14, 16b, 17a, b & d, 18a, 19a & c, 20e,
    22a, 23a–c, 24a, 24d, 25c, 26a, 27b, 30c, 32, 33a, 36b & c, 37a & b,
    38d & e, 39a, 40b, 42a, 44a & b, 46c, 47b & c, 48a & b, 50a, 51a,
    52a & c, 53b, 60a, 66b, 68a & b, 71a & b, 72a, 73a, 75a, 76a, 79b & c, 80
Country Life   48c
The Dean & Chapter of Durham Cathedral   19b
Department of the Environment   9, 43b
Mary Evans Picture Library   65a, 79a
A F Kersting   46b
London Museum   15a, 21b, 73b
Mansell Collection   16c, 24c, 25b, 30a, 45b, 49b, 55a, 77b
National Monuments Record   33c, 34a, 53a
National Portrait Gallery   49a, 77a
Crown Copyright, Public Record Office   13a, 13b, 15b, 29a
Radio Times Hulton Picture Library   5, 11, 16a, 17c, 18b, 20b, c & d,
    21, 25a, 28a, 33b, 34b & c, 46a, 47a, 52b, 58b, 61b, 62a, 64a, 65b, c & d,
    66a, 69a, 72b, 74b, cover
Trinity College, Cambridge   74a
Henry Trivick (from his book *Brasses in Gilt* published by John Baker)   2, 61a,
    69b
Victoria & Albert Museum   20a, 67a
P F White   8, 26b, 27a, 57a, 58a
Nicholas Servian, Woodmansterne Ltd   48d, 55b
Photograph 66c is reproduced by permission of Viscount De l'Isle, VC KG,
    Penshurst Place, Kent
Drawings in this book are by George Tuckwell, J C B Knight, Mary Houston,
    Iris Brooke and others.
Designed by Karen Bowen

Published by A & C Black (Publishers) Ltd
35 Bedford Row London WC1R 4JH

ISBN 0 7136 1421 8 limp
     0 7136 1417 X net

First published in this edition 1974. Reprinted 1975, 1977, 1978 & 1979
© 1974 A & C Black Ltd
Previous editions © 1953, 1961 A & C Black Ltd

Printed in Great Britain by Sir Joseph Causton & Sons Ltd,
London and Eastleigh

Contents

1 The Normans   5
    Norman castles   9
    The Domesday Book   13
    Norman houses   14
    How the people lived   19
    Working on the manor   23
    Holy Days   25

2 Happenings   26

3 The Middle Ages   30
    The monasteries   30
    A monk's day   34
    Friars   35
    Pilgrims and travellers   36
    Obeying the law   39

4 More Happenings   43

5 Town Life in the Middle Ages   50
    Shops   51
    Gilds   53
    Streets in the town   55
    Clothes   59
    Fairs   63
    Plays   64
    Games   65

6 **Homes in the Later Middle Ages** 66
  Manor houses 66
  Merchants' houses 69
  Food and cooking 71
  Poor people's homes 74
  Children 75

7 **Yet More Happenings** 77

  Index 80

Giving a child a ride in a wheelbarrow

This book is about the life of ordinary people in the Middle Ages. It tells you how they built and furnished their homes, how they lived, worked and enjoyed themselves; you will read about their clothes, food, games and punishments.

You will not find very much about kings, queens and battles in this book, but to help you to know who were the rulers, and what were the chief events in the Middle Ages, there are three very short chapters called 'Happenings.' The full stories of these happenings and of the many famous men and women can be found in other history books, but this is a book about everyday people and things.

The Normans 1

The last big invasion of Britain was made by the Normans, from France, led by Duke William of Normandy.

William declared that Edward the Confessor had promised him the crown of England, but as Harold would not give up his kingdom, William and the Normans made ready to attack.

They built ships and filled them with stores, horses and even parts of wooden forts, which were to be put together when they had landed.

Saxon soldiers at Hastings

In 1066 the Normans landed in Sussex, with an army of mounted knights and foot-soldiers. They defeated Harold and the Saxons in a great battle—the Battle of Hastings. Harold and most of the Saxon nobles were killed, and William the Conqueror became King of England.

The Bayeux Tapestry, which was embroidered on a long strip of linen, tells the story of the invasion. On the next two pages are some pictures from it.

Duke William's ships approaching England

Here the Normans are cutting down trees and building their ships.

The Normans go on board their ships.

6

The Normans sail. (Can you see their horses in the ships?)

They land near Hastings.

The battle is very fierce.

At last the Normans win and the Saxons run away.

The Normans who came with William spoke French and dressed like the man and woman on the left.

The knight's helmet had a nose-piece. His coat of mail was called a hauberk. It was a leather jacket with iron rings sewn on to it. At the bottom there was a slit so that he could ride comfortably on horseback. His cloth stockings had leather cross-garters.

The Normans carried swords, battle-axes and lances. Unlike the Saxons, they had a force of archers and the knights charged on horseback.

The lady wore her hair in plaits, sometimes with a veil over it. She wore two tunics (or frocks) with a jewelled belt. Her cloak was fastened with a cord.

A Norman knight and his lady

Actors dressed as knights at a modern tournament

8

Dover Castle. The square keep and the towered inner bailey were built by Henry II

Norman castles

The Saxons hated the Normans, but as they had lost their leaders in the battle, they could not fight on. William was afraid that they might give trouble, so he built castles outside the Saxon towns. In each castle there were Norman soldiers ready to stop the Saxons raising an army.

The first castles had to be built quickly. Each castle was just a wooden tower on a hill, or mound of earth, with a fence round it and a ditch outside.

In time, the wooden towers were replaced by great stone castles. William only built two stone castles —the Tower of London and Colchester Castle.

During the reigns of later Norman kings, many stone castles were built in different parts of the country.

William's early castles were just wooden towers built on a hill

9

Berkhamsted Castle. The mound and the bailey are easily seen

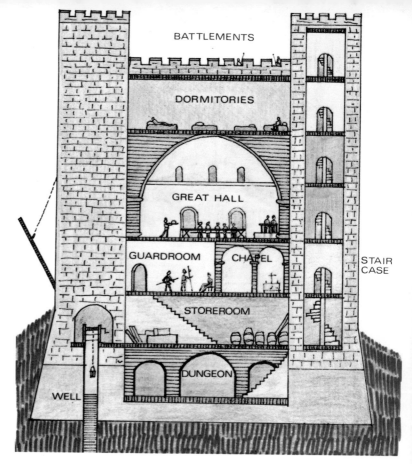

BATTLEMENTS

DORMITORIES

GREAT HALL

GUARDROOM CHAPEL

STOREROOM

STAIR CASE

DUNGEON

WELL

The keep

A gateway with a portcullis

To enter the castle, the Normans crossed over the moat by the drawbridge (which the soldiers could wind up and down from the gatehouse) and went through a great gateway, with thick wooden gates. The gateway also had a portcullis, a strong, pointed iron fence which was drawn upwards to allow people to pass through. When an enemy approached, it was quickly lowered.

Inside the high walls was a big yard called the *outer bailey*. Against the walls were stables and sheds for corn and hay. Cows and sheep were driven into the outer bailey for safety, in troubled times.

The *inner bailey* was a smaller yard, reached by crossing another drawbridge. Here was the Great Tower or *keep*, with walls six metres thick.

At the top of the keep were the battlements, where soldiers kept a look-out over the countryside to see what the Saxons were doing.

Below the battlements were the sleeping-rooms for the lord and his important visitors. Other people slept on benches in the *Great Hall* or lay down on the floor wrapped in their cloaks.

A dungeon

The Great Hall was a long, bare room with small windows in the thick walls. The floor was made of rough oak planks and was covered with rushes. The fire was on a stone slab in the middle, and the smoke had to find its way out through the little windows.

On the next floor were the guard-room and the chapel.

At the very bottom of the keep were store-rooms for food and armour. The well might be here, and also a dungeon for prisoners.

Norman builders at work

The Great Hall of a Norman castle

The staircases were cut in the thickness of the walls and had narrow, stone steps.

There was very little furniture: long tables, which could be taken down to clear a space, benches and two or three chests for clothes and armour. At one end the floor was raised. Here the lord and lady had their meals. The rest of the family and the knights sat lower down.

The binding of Domesday Book. The book has been looked after with great care over the centuries

Domesday Book

William wanted to learn all about his new kingdom and how much it was worth, so he sent his men to find out about every town, village, farm and field in all the land: how big they were, who owned them and how much tax they could pay.

Notes on every place in the country were written down in the Domesday Book. They were written in Latin, in red and black ink. The great book was finished in 1086. It can still be seen in London. The binding in the photograph above was made in Tudor times.

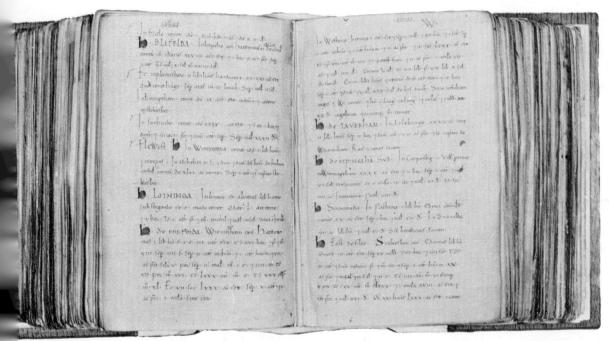

Norman houses

William lent castles to the barons, but he did not like them to build castles for themselves. Some Norman knights were given land and they built stone manor-houses. A manor means an estate, with one or more villages and all the land round about.

Getting out of a coat of mail

Each manor-house had a wall built round it, so that it was like a small castle. The hall, or living-room, was upstairs, for safety. It was reached by a stone staircase outside the house. The windows were bigger than the slits found in castles. They had no glass yet. Wooden shutters kept out the rain and the wind.

A fortified manor house

Downstairs, as in the castles, there were store-rooms and space for the serving men.

The solar

A bronze water jug

By drawing a curtain or screen across one end of the hall, the lord made a small room for himself and his lady. This private room was called the *solar*. They would go there to talk and the lady would sew. They also slept there. Sometimes the solar was an upper room, reached by a ladder, or by an outside staircase.

The lord had a big wooden bed, with a feather mattress, a bolster, linen sheets and a coverlet of fur. As they had no cupboards, the lord and lady hung their clothes on a pole sticking out from the wall. Jewels, money and important manuscripts were kept in a heavy chest. The lord also had a little room cut in the thickness of the walls, called the *treasury*. He kept his wine and other valuables in there.

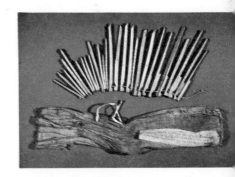

Sticks like this, called tallies were used to record payments. They were kept in the treasury

Stools and the baby's cradle made up the rest of the furniture, and there was a fireplace against one of the outer walls.

There was often a pet hawk in the solar, or a squirrel in a cage. Hunting dogs were kept at every manor-house.

A baker's oven

The kitchen was a separate building, across the yard, so the food was not very hot by the time it reached the hall. Later on, the lord made a covered way from his kitchen, and later still, the kitchen became part of the house.

In the kitchen

The lord liked good food and he had cooks and scullions to prepare it.

At this time a lot of meat was eaten: beef, mutton, pork and venison (deer), and all kinds of birds and fish, especially herrings and eels. Poor people lived mainly on vegetables: peas, beans and cabbages, with a piece of bacon now and then.

Eating a picnic during a hunt

The kitchen of a manor house prepared food for many people

16

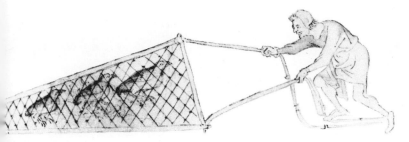

Trapping birds

There was never enough hay for all the cattle in winter, so most of them were killed in the autumn. The meat was then put into barrels of salt water to save it from going bad. Everyone soon grew tired of eating salt meat and herrings, and they added spices to make their food more tasty.

Hawking

The lord and his knights would go hunting and hawking to get fresh meat. Roast chickens, geese and swans were popular dishes, and even peacocks were served if the king came on a visit.

There were other huts in the manor-yard besides the kitchen. There was the brew-house, where the ale and mead were made, the pantry, the dairy and the buttery. As there were no shops, nearly everything was made at the manor-house.

Milking

Trapping rabbits with a ferret

17

The lord at his table

A jester

The lord had his dinner at 10 o'clock in the morning and his supper about 6 o'clock.

His table stood higher than the rest. In the centre it had a large salt-cellar. Ordinary people sat lower down in the hall, 'below the salt.'

At the lord's table there was French wine to drink, as well as ale. Glasses and goblets were now used for drinking. There were plates, knives and spoons, but no forks.

A page from another noble family waited on the lord and his guests. Before and after dinner, he brought them a bowl of water and a napkin, so that they could wash their hands.

After dinner, the minstrels played and sang, and the jester made everyone laugh.

How the people lived

The king was the ruler of the kingdom. He owned the land and forests. He gave land to the barons and to the abbots, who knelt down and, placing their hands in his, promised to be his men, to obey his laws and to give him soldiers and money when they were needed. Thus, the Normans said that every man had an overlord.

Barons, knights and abbots were the lords of the manor. They kept some land for themselves and gave the rest to the villeins (or peasants).

Every villein also did homage to his lord. This means that he promised to be his man and to obey the customs of the manor. He also promised, in return for some land, to work on the lord's land and to give him various things.

Doing homage

Using a harrow on the land

19

Sowing seed in October

A villein in Norman times might have to do these things:

Plough 4 acres (about $1\frac{1}{2}$ hectares) for his lord in the spring. Lend him 2 oxen for 7 days a year. Work 3 days a week on his domain (land). Pay 1 hen and 16 eggs each year. Bring 1 cartload of wood from the forest to the manor-house. Grind his corn in the lord's mill. Pay a fine if his daughter married. Pay a fine if he sent his son to school at the monastery.

He could never leave the village except to carry a message or to go with his lord to war.

On some manors the customs and payments were a little different. But, generally, a man who held a lot of land had to do more work for the lord and make more payment than a villein who only held a little land.

Storing corn

Early mills were all watermills

Sickles and pruning knives

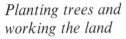

Planting trees and working the land

All this was written down in the Court Roll and the lord's *steward* and the village *reeve* saw that it was carried out. Any villein who disobeyed was brought to the Manor Court to pay a fine.

A villein who was able to save enough money, liked to pay a rent for his land instead of doing 'week-work' for the lord. Then he could spend all his time on his own land. He was now a freeman, and no longer a serf.

A villein's cott or hut

If the lord was cruel, or if a villein had committed a crime, he might run away to the forest and become an outlaw. Everyone was supposed to arrest or kill an outlaw, but if he could reach a town and not be caught for a year and a day, he became a freeman.

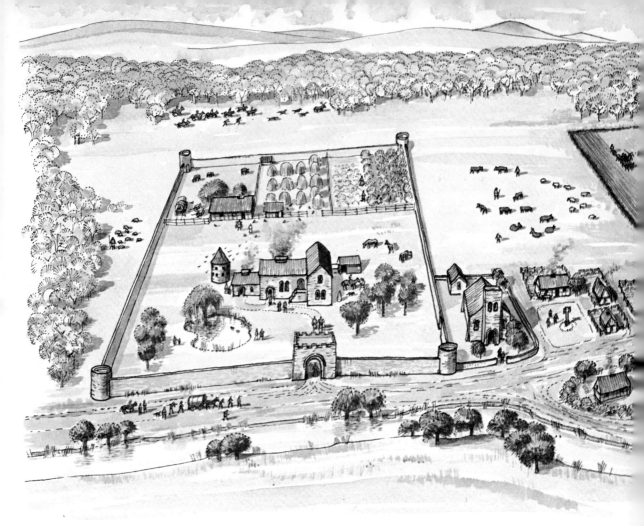

A typical village

Storing the harvest

In the village, besides the stone manor-house, there were the church and the cross, the priest's house and twenty or thirty huts for the villeins. These were made of wattle and daub (wicker and mud) with thatched roofs. The smoky little huts had a fire in the middle of their one room.

Most manors had three large fields, one growing wheat, one barley and one resting (lying fallow). In the wheat and barley fields there would also be some oats, rye, beans and peas. Each field was shared out into strips of land, with little grass paths between. This meant that everyone had a share of good and bad land.

Working on the manor

The corn was taken to the lord's mill to be ground into flour. The villeins had to pay for this.

Bringing corn to the mill

Outside the fields was the common-land, where the animals could graze. Each one was marked with its owner's mark. If a cow strayed, it was put in a little yard with a fence round it, called the pound. The owner had to pay two pence to get it back.

Down by the river was the meadow-land, where the long grass was cut and dried to provide hay in winter.

Ploughing with oxen

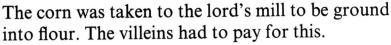

The women worked hard, making butter and looking after the little gardens of peas, beans and cabbages. (There were no potatoes yet.) In the evenings they spun sheep's wool into thread and wove it into rough cloth.

Children looked after the animals and scared birds from the crops.

It was a very hard life for the villeins, who grumbled continuously about their tasks, especially at haymaking and harvest, when they had to do extra work for the lord. The reeve was allowed to beat them if they did not work hard.

The way in which people lived on the manor is called the *Feudal System*.

At Christmas people dressed up as mummers

Holy Days

The villagers enjoyed many Holy Days, such as Christmas Day, May-day and Midsummer Eve. The villeins went to church on these days, and afterwards sports and dancing were held on the green, with races, wrestling, jumping, archery and throwing lances. People danced round the maypole and afterwards went to the ale house and made merry.

At Christmas everyone went to the manor-house for a feast in the hall. There were rough games afterwards, like *hoodman blind*.

Dancing round the maypole

Wrestling

2 Happenings

William I was the first Norman king. He was strong and wise, and he made the barons obey him. He could be cruel, and when the Saxons in the north rebelled, he punished them with fire and death, but when people obeyed him, William treated them fairly.

Hereward the Wake was the leader of a Saxon rebellion. With a company of other rebels he hid in the marshes of Ely, but although William's soldiers found his hiding-place, he escaped.

William Rufus, the Red-Head, was the next king. He was killed by an arrow when hunting.

Henry I, his brother, kept peace and order in the land. Trade was good. Many churches and monasteries were built and towns grew larger. The Normans and Saxons were now learning to live together in peace.

When Henry I died the nobles would not have his daughter, Matilda, as queen. Stephen, her cousin, was made king instead. Then there was a civil war between the barons, and people went in fear of their lives.

The barons built castles for themselves and would not obey the king. Many cruel things were done and men said, 'God and his Saints slept.'

Orford Castle, built by Henry II

Henry II (1154) was a strong king. He made the barons obey him and pulled down some of the castles they had built without royal permission.

He also tried to force the clergy, who were very powerful, to obey his rules. Thomas à Becket, Archbishop of Canterbury, would not do so and for a long time he argued with the king.

Henry, in a fit of temper, caused some of his knights to kill Becket in Canterbury Cathedral, but he was sorry for this deed and did penance by walking through the city and by being whipped in the Cathedral.

People called Becket Saint Thomas and went as pilgrims to Canterbury, to pray at his tomb.

A small Norman church

Henry II and Becket

The murder of Becket

27

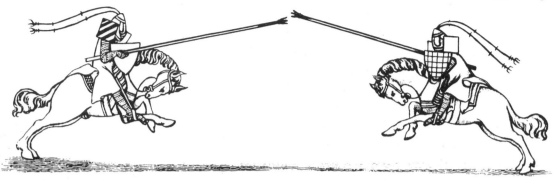

Jousting

The barons loved fighting and often had tournaments for sport in their castle-yards. So, when Richard I, the Lion-Heart, took an army to the Holy Land for the Third Crusade, they followed him eagerly.

For 200 years, French, German, and English knights went on Crusades. They captured Jerusalem from the Turks and ruled most of the Holy Land for a time. But they were always quarrelling among themselves.

Saladin, a great leader, recaptured Jerusalem in 1187 and although Richard I defeated Saladin, he could not win Jerusalem back.

A siege

When they came home, the Crusaders brought back new ideas about building, warfare and castles. They also brought carpets, sugar, and fruits such as lemons. In the East, they had learned about tars, medicine and mathematics.

King John quarrelled with the barons and the clergy. The Pope said that he must be turned off the throne but John made his peace and continued to do as he pleased. In 1215, the barons forced him to put his seal to Magna Carta, a charter or ist of their rights. His promise to rule well was soon broken.

Robin Hood and his Merry Men are said to have lived at this time in Sherwood Forest. They were outlaws who had run away from their lords. Robin Hood was a popular hero, for he robbed the rich to help the poor.

There were also many bands of robbers who hid in the forests and robbed travellers.

Magna Carta

Robin Hood

A crusader ship

3 The Middle Ages

A bishop

By this time the Normans had settled down with the Saxons and had become the English people.

The monasteries

Although there was much fighting and cruelty people were very religious. The bishops and abbots were as powerful as the barons. They owned numerous manors, because when rich men died, they left money and land to the monasteries, asking the monks to pray for their souls.

Building the abbey of St Albans

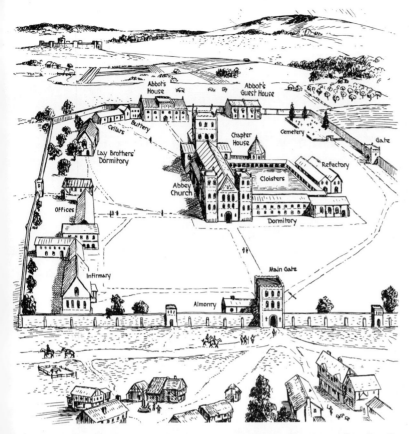

If you remember that many of the great cathedrals were once the monastery churches, then you can guess how big an abbey was, for there were many other buildings as well: the almonry, where money and food were given to the poor; the cloisters, where the monks could walk up and down in all weathers, and where they taught the young monks; and the infirmary, where the monks looked after sick people.

Feeding the poor

In the refectory (dining-room) of a large abbey, scores of monks and visitors could sit down to dinner at one time.

There were many monasteries in different parts of the country, each in the charge of an abbot or a prior who was lord over towns and villages in the neighbourhood.

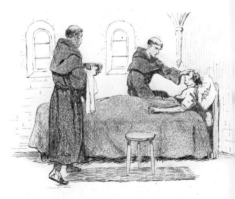

Looking after the sick

Fishing

Building

The Monks were:
the Abbot
the Prior (his chief helper)
the Sub-Prior (his second helper)
the Sacristan, who looked after the church
the Hospitaller, who looked after visitors
the Infirmarian, who looked after the sick
the Almoner, who helped the poor
the ordinary monks, who obeyed these chief monks, and also did gardening, farming, fishing and building, as well as praying and singing hymns in Latin.

In some monasteries, there were also lay-brothers who were chosen to help with the farm work. They lived at the abbey but did not spend as much time in church as the *choir monks*.

Lastly, there were the novices, who were boys learning to be monks.

A new monk has his head shaved; this is called a tonsure

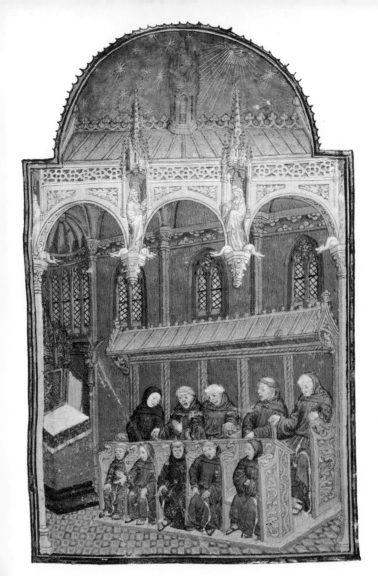

Praying together was an important part of religious life

The cellarer looked after the food and drink – but sometimes he helped himself

The monasteries did much good work: they looked after sick people, for there were no hospitals in these days; they helped the poor, gave shelter to travellers, and taught reading and writing.

Many churches were built by the monks in Norman times. They built for the glory of God. Their work took many, many years to finish and much of it can still be seen in our cathedrals.

On the right is Durham Cathedral. Notice the Norman arches, which are rounded at the top, and the decorated columns.

Durham Cathedral

A monk's day

Long before daylight, all the monks went down to the great church to say prayers called Matins. The next service, Lauds, lasted until 2 or 3 o'clock.

The monks went back to bed until daybreak; then came a service called Prime, followed by a light breakfast of bread with wine or ale.

At 8 o'clock in the Chapter House, the abbot told the monks their duties for the day and any who had misbehaved were punished.

After Chapter they walked awhile in the cloisters.

At 10 o'clock came the most important service, High Mass, followed by dinner in the Refectory, when the monks did not speak but were read to from the Bible or a holy book.

After dinner came the work of the day—gardening, farming, writing, building or fishing.

Evening prayers called Vespers were said before supper and at 7 or 8 o'clock came the last service, Compline, after which the monks went to bed.

Soon after midnight, the bell rang for the next day to begin.

The Chapter house at Salisbury

Writing a manuscript

A service

Friars

There were also friars, who wandered from place to place, preaching and helping the poor: Black Friars, White Friars, and best loved, the Grey Friars who tried, like St. Francis, to be kind and gentle. They looked after the sick and became famous for their skill and knowledge in curing illness.

A Lollard preaching

There were also nuns, who lived together in religious houses called nunneries. They led much the same kind of lives as the monks, attending church services, teaching children and doing needlework.

John Wycliffe was a famous preacher, who tried to make men lead better lives. His followers, called Lollards, used to preach on the village green, or by the town cross.

The friars went from village to village

35

A company of pilgrims at supper at an inn

A lady sometimes rode behind a man

Pilgrims and travellers

Everyone tried to go on a pilgrimage, to say prayers at a holy place, at least once in his life. Pilgrims went to Canterbury, St. Albans, Glastonbury and other holy places as far away as Spain, Rome and the Holy Land. A party of people would set off together. It made a holiday for them.

Pilgrims usually walked on their long journeys. A pilgrim might wear a cockle-shell in his hat to show that he had been to Compostella in Spain. He was often called a palmer, because he carried a piece of palm from the Holy Land.

A coach, drawn by five horses

Carts were used to take criminals to execution

A small carriage

Noble ladies rode in a clumsy coach pulled by five or six horses, or they were carried by servants in a litter. Rich travellers rode on horseback, and ladies on a pillion seat behind a servant. It was disgraceful to ride in a cart, because that was how prisoners were taken to be executed.

Merchants took their goods from town to town on pack-horses or mules.

The roads were very bad indeed because no one mended them. They were only rough tracks. Sometimes a farmer was fined for ploughing up the King's Highway.

Packhorses

The Wife of Bath, a nun and the nuns' priest, from Chaucer's Canterbury Tales

Geoffrey Chaucer wrote down the stories which some pilgrims told on the way to St. Thomas à Becket's tomb. They are called *The Canterbury Tales*.

Journeys were slow and dangerous, because of robbers. Travellers stayed the night at inns, which had a bunch of holly outside for a sign. It took two or three days to go from London to Canterbury.

Geoffrey Chaucer

Pilgrims used seals like this to show that they had been on pilgrimage

The Middle Ages

Obeying the law

There were no law courts yet. A man was punished at the Manor Court by his lord, who would make him pay a fine for such crimes as letting his beasts wander in the corn, or for taking firewood. He could also be tried at the Shire Moot by the Sheriff.

There were some old Saxons customs still in use.

A savage medieval punishment

If a man was accused of a crime, he might suffer *ordeal by fire*. He had to carry a piece of red-hot iron for three paces. His hand was then bound up. If, when it was undone three days later, there were no blisters, he was innocent, but if he had blisters he was punished or killed.

Ordeal by water meant that he was tied up and thrown into the river. If he floated he was guilty of the crime.

Ordeal by fire

39

Trial by combat

Ordeal by combat was introduced by the Normans. A noble had to fight the man who accused him. Both men had shields and special axes; they might fight all day until one cried 'Craven'—then he was put to death. Sometimes a noble got a champion to fight for him.

Henry II made new laws and stopped most of these cruel ways of trial. He ordered *trial by jury*. This meant that twelve good men came to swear what they knew about the man who was accused.

As there were no police, the king's laws were often broken, and if the king was weak, the barons did as they liked. Men sometimes bribed others to say things which were not true.

At this time there were many strange punishments. Cheats and thieves were put in the pillory, or had to sit all day in the stocks, so that everyone laughed at them and pelted them with rubbish.

A friar and a woman in the stocks

A fishmonger who sold bad fish

A baker who made poor bread would be dragged on a sledge, with a loaf tied to his neck.

If a fishmonger sold bad fish, he would be taken round the town with stinking fish hanging from his neck.

A priest being punished

Sometimes a man's hair was cut off and he was marched to prison with 'minstrelsy' (music and drums). A bad priest would have to ride through the streets sitting facing his horse's tail and wearing a paper crown.

A woman who nagged her husband was called a 'scold'. She was tied on a chair and dipped in the river. This chair was called the *ducking stool*.

She might also have to wear a *scold's bridle,* which had a piece of iron to go in the mouth to keep her tongue down.

The ducking stool

41

A nobleman beheaded in public

There was no torture in England at this time, but sometimes ears or hands were cut off and noses slit for punishment. Rogues were whipped and murderers hanged in public for everybody to see, but nobles could choose to be beheaded.

In the towns, the mayor and aldermen were supposed to keep order, and they paid the *common sergeant* and the *watchman* to do the work for them.

After curfew (which means 'cover fire' and was a law made by the Normans to make the Saxons go to bed early), no one was allowed to be out on the streets, or the watchman would arrest them. Curfew was at 8 o'clock in the winter and 9 o'clock in the summer.

More Happenings 4

Simon de Montfort

King John died whilst at war with the barons and his nine-year-old son became Henry III. When he grew up, Henry ruled badly and offended the barons. They were led by Simon de Montfort, who called the first Parliament in 1265. It was a meeting of knights, barons and citizens from some of the towns.

Edward I came next. He was a strong king who restored order. He conquered Wales, for the Welsh people had never obeyed the Normans, and he built some fine castles like Harlech, which can still be seen today.

He also tried to conquer the Scots, but he did not succeed. He was called Edward Long-shanks, Hammer of the Scots.

Harlech Castle, built by Edward I

A battle, about the year 1350

Edward II was a weak king, and the Scots, led by Robert Bruce, defeated the English at the Battle of Bannockburn.

Then came Edward III, who spent much of his time fighting the French. His son was the Black Prince. The English army led by the King or Prince, was made up of knights or nobles, with their squires and pages, and the foot-soldiers, who were villeins, armed with longbows.

A page was a noble's son, who at the age of seven was sent to live at another castle, to wait at table and to learn manners. When he was fourteen, he became a squire and learnt to fight and to help his knight with his armour. One day, if he proved brave in battle, he would win his spurs and become a knight.

Sir Geoffrey Luttrell of Lincolnshire setting off for war

More Happenings

The nobles were fond of melées and jousts, which were held at court. Two knights, separated by a low fence, charged each other at top speed, each trying to unseat the other with his lance.

The English longbow could kill a man in armour nearly 200 metres away. The bow was as long as the archer. It was made of yew and the bowstring of hemp or flax. The arrow was a *cloth-yard* (just under a metre) long and was made of ash with grey goose feathers. The archer wore a bracer or laced leather sleeve on his left arm.

The French used crossbows, which were more powerful than longbows, but as they had to be wound up, they could not be fired as quickly.

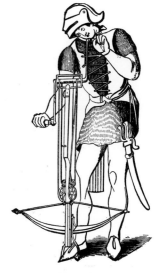

A crossbowman

A tournament

An army on the march

Practising archery

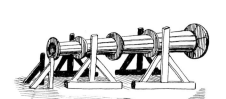

The villeins, who followed their lords to battle, carried longbows. They were good archers, because Edward made a law that all men must practise archery at the butts in the village church-yards, instead of playing football.

Towns and castles were so strong that a siege lasted a long time, and if the attackers could not batter a hole in the walls, they surrounded it and starved the people inside. This was how Edward III captured Calais.

Sieges could also be dangerous for the attackers, because of a disease known as *camp fever*. Both the Black Prince and Henry V died of illnesses caused by unhealthy conditions in camp.

Edward III

The siege of Calais

Tending sheep

A sheep-pen

During the French Wars a terrible disease came from the East called the Black Death (1348). Thousands of people died and some villages and manors had hardly anyone left alive.

There were not enough men to plough the land and sow the corn, so the lords of the manor let grass grow instead. They kept many sheep on it, because their wool was valuable.

Sheep are loaded on board ship to be sold abroad

Spinning wool and dyeing cloth

English wool was very good and much of it was sold to Flanders (Belgium). Weavers from Flanders came to live in England and wool towns in Norfolk, Suffolk and Gloucestershire became very rich. Merchants built fine houses and churches.

When so many sheep were kept, a large number of villeins lost their strips of land. They became poor and unhappy and said 'Sheep eat men.'

A merchant's house in Essex

Church at Lavenham, a wool town in Suffolk

The Black Prince was never king. He died, worn out with much fighting, and his son, Richard II, was only a boy when he became king.

After the Black Death, the villeins grumbled because there were new laws which forced them to stay with their lord and work much harder. This was necessary because so many people had died. They also had to pay heavy taxes, and at this they rebelled. Led by Wat Tyler and John Ball, a poor preacher, they marched angrily to London. This was the Peasants' Revolt.

In this old picture, the young king, Richard II, is promising to help the peasants, but these promises were not kept. Later on the nobles rebelled against him and they made his cousin king in his place, as Henry IV.

Richard II

In 'Happenings' you have read a lot about the kings. This is because the king was the real ruler of England in the Middle Ages. If he was weak, or a boy-king, he could not keep the barons in order and their quarrels and private wars made life wretched and dangerous for everybody.

Richard II going to meet the peasants. His promises to them were not kept

5 Town Life in the Middle Ages

A street in a medieval town

After the Normans came, towns grew bigger, especially London, which was now the capital of England. Even so, they were not very large towns, for there were fewer people in all England than there are in London today. The streets were narrow and the houses were built close together.

Round each town there was a thick wall, for safety against enemies, and the town gates were locked every night at sunset.

London about 1430, showing the Tower and London Bridge

The townsfolk were freemen who had paid their lord a sum of money to be free and they had to look after themselves. They chose a mayor, who, with the help of his aldermen, ruled the town. Every town had its own laws and punishments. The mayor told the people what they must do through the town crier, who called out messages and news at the market cross.

A town crier

Shops

There were shops in the town, but they were not large buildings with glass windows. When a man had things to sell—shoes or cloth, candles or pewter cups—he put them on a stall in the front of his downstairs room and went on working at his trade. People who did not live in the town often sold their wares outside its walls.

In this picture an artist of the Middle Ages has tried to show town life of his time. Notice the stalls outside the walls, the changing of foreign money in the gateway, the style of clothes and the artist's way of showing a scene inside a house

51

Blacksmiths at work

A baker and his wife

Some towns, especially in Italy and Flanders, were like little states. They had their own laws, taxes, and trading rights. For a sum of money, the townsmen might get a charter from the king; then they could have a mayor and a market.

Shopkeepers nearly always sold the goods which they made themselves, and the men who made one kind of thing lived in the same street. There were streets called Candlemakers' Row, Butchers' Row, Glovers' Row, Ironmongers' Lane, Milk Street, Silver Street and Honey Lane.

They hung the sign of their trade outside their shop—a fish, a boot or a pair of scissors. Some of these old signs can still be found occasionally. Names were not written over the shops because few people could read.

A town bridge

A medieval shop

A prosperous merchant

Gilds

The craftsmen joined together in gilds (or guilds), which were meetings of men in the same trade. There were the Tailors' Gild, the Goldsmiths' Gild and many others.

These gilds did good work. They made sure that their members charged honest prices and used good materials.

They helped widows and orphans, and it is known that the Carpenters' Gild gave fourteen pence a week to a member who was ill.

The gilds also helped to look after the town church and to pay money for candles on the altar, for building a new chapel or for a school. Sometimes they gave money to mend the town bridge.

The Gildhall at Thaxted in Essex

A man had to prove his skill before being allowed to join a gild

Football in the streets was a rough game

When a boy was about fourteen, he might become an apprentice, which means that he would learn a trade for seven years. He went to live with his master, to learn how to make clothes, or armour, or whatever his master made. At night he slept in the shop. He would also help to sell the goods, crying out to passers-by, 'What d'ye lack? What d'ye lack?'

The apprentice boys were full of fun and liked to play football, handball, marbles and tops, but their masters would beat them if they dodged their work. They also liked archery and the cruel sport of bull-baiting, in which fierce dogs were set to attack a bull.

Streets in the town

Every town had many churches, some of them built with money given by rich merchants. Arches and doorways were now more pointed than those built by the Normans. People were religious and no one missed going to church on Sundays and holy days.

A worker in a mint. Coins were minted in many towns in Britain

In the middle of the town was the market-place and the town cross, where the king's herald or the town crier called out the news, and friars or Lollards preached. Here, too, were the stocks and the pillory.

The narrow streets were very dirty. There were cobbles outside the shops, but in the middle of the road was a kind of gutter into which everyone threw their rubbish, even sweepings from the stables, dead dogs and other smelly things.

A cathedral door

Salisbury Cathedral

The mayor was always trying to get the streets cleaner. He would punish butchers for killing animals outside their shops and for throwing down the parts which no one could eat.

People threw dirty water from upstairs windows, and pigs and chickens wandered in and out of the rubbish looking for food.

Pigs were a great nuisance and some people even made pig-sties in the streets and alleys, until a law was made which said 'He who shall wish to feed a pig, must feed it in his house.' Any pig found wandering could be killed though the owner could pay a fine to get it back

Medieval buildings in Warwick. Beneath the gild chapel, you can see the town gate

The townsfolk did not like carts with iron wheels, because they broke up the paving stones, so sledges were often used instead.

Travelling merchants had to pay a toll before they could come inside the town gates. It cost more for a big cart loaded with mill-stones, than for a small cart which would damage the road less.

A water carrier

Water had to be fetched from the river or drawn from wells in the town. It could also be bought from water-carriers, who took it round the streets in carts or buckets.

For a long time castles and monasteries had had lead water-pipes. Now they were laid in some streets. People used to cut the pipes to get water for themselves, which made the mayor angry.

As the houses were very close together and made partly of wood, everyone was frightened of fire. Outside some of the houses hung leather fire buckets and big hooks for pulling off burning thatch.

Fire hook and leather bucket

A carved wooden head on a medieval house

Doctors had no cure for leprosy

Houses were of many different shapes and sizes, because people built houses just as they pleased. Land was scarce inside the small walled towns, so if a merchant wanted to make his house bigger, he added another storey on top.

In these days there were lepers, people who had a terrible disease called leprosy, which, it is thought, the Crusaders brought back from the East. They were not allowed to live in the towns. Food was left for them outside the town walls and kind people gave money to build special houses for them to live in. Lepers carried a bell to warn passers-by and cried out 'Unclean, unclean.'

There were also many beggars wandering from town to town. They were rough, wild men who often robbed people to get food and clothing.

Beggars

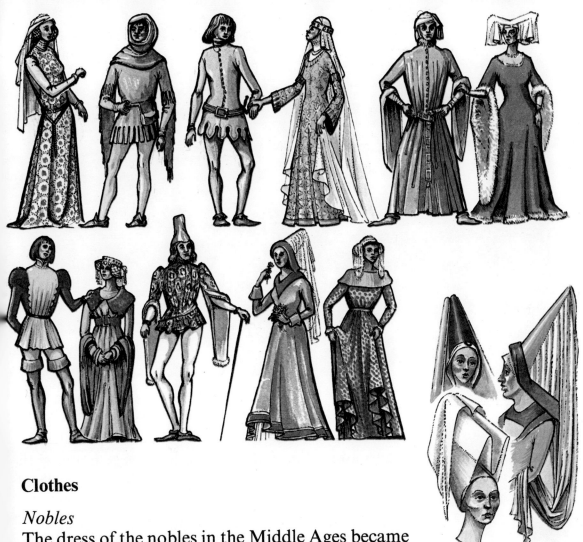

Clothes

Nobles

The dress of the nobles in the Middle Ages became very gay and brightly coloured. The courtiers wore long gowns with wide sleeves, which touched the ground, or short pleated top-coats, belted and edged with fur. They pulled their waists in tightly and padded their chests.

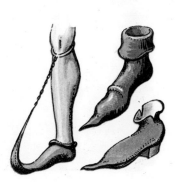

They wore stockings, often with different coloured legs, and shoes so pointed that sometimes the points were curled up and, fastened to a garter below the knee, by a silver chain. Men wore hats both indoors and out. They would keep their hats on when eating their dinner.

Ladies of the Court

The ladies wore tall pointed hats made of gold and silver tissue, with a velvet or fur roll round them and a large veil. Some hats were made with two horns; others were jewelled. Dresses were long and full and the under-dress (the cotte) hardly showed at all; it was becoming a petticoat.

Merchants

Merchants and their wives usually wore long dark gowns because they were not allowed to dress in such bright colours as the nobles.

Apprentices

Apprentices were forbidden to wear fine clothes or to try to copy the upper classes.

Children

Children were dressed like grown-ups. A noble boy's long boots would be made of soft leather. Small children wore nothing but a tunic in summer.

A merchant and his wife

Knights

For jousting, knights wore their full armour and sometimes a coloured surcoat on top. Their helmets were often topped by a crest—a bird or animal made of wood and leather.

The poor folk

These still wore rough belted tunics, leggings and wooden clogs, or shoes of thick cloth. Peasant women wore long dresses of coarse cloth and hoods or wimples on their heads. The children had short tunics and were bare-footed.

Nearly all men at this time wore a useful garment called a capuchon, which was a hood with a short cape. Later on, the merchants twisted it up on their heads like a turban. Both men and women wore cloaks

A brass rubbing showing a knight and his lady. Notice how his hair was cut as a padding under the helmet

The clothing of the poor

Ladies out hunting

Nobles carried daggers, and pouches at their belts (instead of pockets) and sometimes a little whip for beating servants. The ladies had handbags.

Shoes were narrow and pointed, but heels were not yet in use.

Clothes were mostly made of woollen cloth, some of it very fine, and linen. Noble ladies bought silk from Italy and heavy material called damask, which originally came from Damascus. Fur was very popular for linings and trimmings.

Fairs

Great fairs were held (especially at Northampton and Winchester) to which traders from all parts, even from across the sea, came to bring their goods. Such a fair as St. Giles's Fair at Winchester would last for sixteen days. The fairground was just outside the walls, in a big field.

At the fair there would be nobles and poor men, beggars and thieves, travellers from foreign lands and merchants arriving with pack-horses.

All kinds of goods were on sale: leather, wine, bales of wool, beautiful glasses from Italy and mirrors from France, spices from the East, carpets and oranges, silks and velvets for the rich people and parchment for the monks to write on.

There were other fine sights to see: jugglers balancing swords and swallowing fire, mummers and musicians, monkeys and dancing bears.

A dancing bear

A medieval fair

Plays

In the Middle Ages people enjoyed watching plays, which, at first, were acted in the church porch. This was how the priests taught the people Bible stories.

Sometimes these religious plays were acted on a cart which went round the town. They were called Miracle Plays.

A Miracle Play, acted on a cart in the streets

Then there were Gild Plays, each acted by members of one gild. The gilds chose stories which suited their trade; the fishmongers, for instance, would act *Jonah and the Whale*.

Chess, bowls and cards were favourite pastimes

Games

Children and grown-ups played games, some of which were rather rough. In *hot cockles* one player knelt down blindfold and the others gave him hard whacks until he guessed who it was. *Hoodman blind* was like our blindman's buff, except that one must hit the blind man with a knotted capuchon (hood).

Boys also played *hoop and hide, hide and seek, fillip the toad, ninepins, stoolball* and *barley-break*.

Grown-ups played these games and also football, which was later stopped because so many people were hurt or killed. They liked dancing, and we know they played chess and draughts. The sons of nobles played with jointed soldiers, and girls had dolls.

Fishing

6 Homes in the Later Middle Ages

Manor houses

The first manor-houses, in Norman times, were built with the hall upstairs for safety and an outside staircase. They were draughty and uncomfortable. The only other room, besides the hall, was the lord's solar, or bedroom.

In later days the hall was downstairs and the manor-houses were made more comfortable. There were now several bedrooms, and these were reached by staircases inside the house. Wooden screens kept off draughts from the door.

Large manor-houses had a gallery in the great hall for musicians, who would play to the lord and his noble guests. The king and his court were always travelling about the country, staying first with one lord and then with another.

A gittern, the oldest surviving English musical instrument

The Great Hall at Penshurst Place

The inside walls, instead of being bare stone, were now covered with wooden panels, painted in gay colours, or with tapestries like the one in the picture, which covered much of the walls from floor to ceiling. Many of these were woven in Flanders. The best came from a town called Arras.

The floors had tiles and rush mats, in place of dirty rushes, but only the richest people had carpets and these were hung on the walls or spread on tables.

Glass was now being put into the window spaces in nobles' houses. The glass was very costly and was fitted into frames, which were taken down when the lord went away.

A tapestry, woven at Tournai

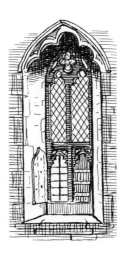

Inside a nobleman's house

The noble family now had a smaller room near the hall called the winter parlour. This was cosier in the winter and was used when there were no important visitors. There was a big fireplace, with a fire of logs on the wide hearth, but there was still very little furniture, even in the richest homes.

The manor-houses in the country still needed a thick wall around them and a moat, and all men, except monks and clerks, had to be ready to fight an unfriendly baron.

The kitchen was now joined to the house by a covered way, and so were the pantry (bread store) and buttery (ale and wine store).

Geoffrey Kidwelly, a merchant. Notice his purse and prayer beads

We first hear of flower, gardens about this time, which means that life was a little more peaceful. You can see on this page one of the earliest pictures of a town garden.

Merchants' houses

In the towns, merchants lived above their shops and workrooms. They had a fine panelled living-room with a large fireplace, and if they were rich, glass filled the window spaces. On the floor they had rush mats. Their servants hung fresh green branches on the walls for decoration.

The apprentices, who always lived in their masters' house, slept in the shop, often curled up under the counter.

Inside a merchant's house

This merchant and his guest are in the living-room. They have finished dinner and are now discussing business. Notice the wide bench on which they are sitting, with its cushioned seat and high wooden back.

The merchant's solar, or bedroom, was over the living-room. It jutted out over the street. (The servants could easily throw water down into the street gutter from here.)

The bed was the most important piece of furniture, with its feather mattress, and its curtains to pull all round at night.

A bedroom

There was also a cradle for the baby and, under the big bed, a truckle bed on wheels to be pulled out at night for a lady's maid-servant.

A strong box, or coffer, was often kept at the foot of the bed, in which were stored money, jewels and important papers, for there were no banks where a man might keep his valuables safely.

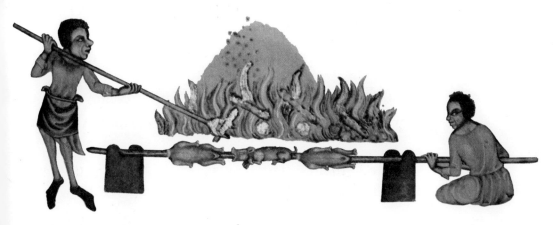

Food and cooking

Cooking on a spit

Every manor-house had a large kitchen with several fireplaces. There were many cooks and scullion boys, each with their own special job. They had to prepare meals for all the people who lived in a manor-house—perhaps fifty persons, and visitors also.

A water-jug

Ovens came into use in kitchens at this time

Joints of fresh meat, perhaps venison, chickens and geese, were roasted in front of the fire on a spit, which was turned by a scullion boy. When the birds were done, they were served at table, from the spit.

Salted meat, which was eaten in winter, was boiled in large cauldrons, and served as stew.

At this time, ovens came into use. An oven was a big space in the thick wall, with an iron door. A bundle of faggots was put inside and lighted. When all the sticks had burned out, the door was opened and the ashes were raked to one side. Bread, pies and cakes were put inside. The door was shut and by the time the oven was cool, they were cooked.

In smaller houses and in peasants' cottages, they made an oven by pushing aside the ashes of a hot wood fire, and putting the pie down on the hearth under an iron cover. Hot ashes were then piled on top.

Meat, cheese and bread were the chief foods. (There were still no potatoes.) Herrings, eels and salted fish were very common in winter. Spices, such as ginger, cinnamon and saffron, were used by the rich to make their food more tasty.

Cooking in a cauldron

The lord of the manor at table

Cider, beer and wine were drunk, and even the children had beer for breakfast. Fruit was now more popular and apples, pears, peaches and plums were grown. Grape vines often covered the sunny monastery walls, and dates, figs and oranges could be bought at the fair.

People were very big eaters, as you can see from this menu:

First course: lamprey, codling, mutton, chicken, goose, dove, worts (vegetables) and pastry.

Second course: eels, sea horses, lamb, duck, quail, goldfinches and pie.

On the tables there were now cloths, spoons and knives, a silver salt-cellar and silver or pewter dishes and jugs. Even so, round thick slices of bread called *trenchers* were sometimes used for plates.

Dinner was at 10 or 11 o'clock in the morning and lasted a long time.

Medieval jugs

73

Ploughing

Poor people's homes

The peasants' homes, or cotts, were made of wattle and daub, with oak beams and thatched roofs. There were two rooms, the bower or bedroom, and a larger living-room, which often had a stable at one end. The fire-place, with a stone slab or iron fireback, was now against the wall.

It had a rough chimney-hood to lead the smoke out. The peasants had very little furniture. Their food was still bread, vegetables, eggs and sometimes a little meat. They began work when it was light, and went on until sunset, except on holy days, when everyone enjoyed themselves.

Clearing land for farming

A page serving at table

An engaged couple

Children

In these days parents were very strict with their children and beat them for any misbehaviour. Even when they were quite grown up, they could not do as they wished, but had to obey their parents.

The sons of nobles were sent to another lord when they were seven years old. They lived in his manor or castle as pages, learning good manners and how to wait at table.

Using a spinning wheel

The girls learned how to manage a big house and how to make medicines from herbs, called simples. They also did beautiful needlework and spinning, and in time the unmarried ones were called spinsters.

Parents arranged marriages without asking their children. Girls were often married at fourteen or sixteen, and it was quite a disgrace to be unmarried at twenty.

75

A school

Looking after the sheep

There were a few schools (such as Eton and Winchester), but rich men's children were more often taught at home by a tutor, who was a monk or family priest. He took prayers at home and usually wrote all the letters.

Peasants' children did not go to school, but a few were sent to the monastery as novices, to be trained as monks.

Sometimes priests taught the children Bible stories in the church porch.

By the time peasants' children were seven years old, most of them were minding the animals and helping their fathers. Only rarely was a poor boy allowed to go to the monastery school to learn to read and write. If he was lucky, he might become a clerk or bailiff on the manor.

Yet More Happenings 7

Henry IV, who had taken away the crown from Richard II, tried to rule the country well and the barons were more peaceable.

His son, Henry V, was a famous soldier-king. He restarted the war with France, which had gone on for so long that it was known as the Hundred Years' War.

Henry took a small army across the Channel and attacked the French. He won a remarkable victory at Agincourt in 1415, when the English archers proved their skill against the heavily armed French knights.

Henry V

A sea battle in the Hundred Years War

English archers at Agincourt

Joan of Arc

The archers stood behind a row of pointed stakes. The French knights on horseback charged, but they could not pass the stakes and their horses stumbled and fell. The archers fired arrows from their long-bows, and the arrows fell like rain among the French.

After this victory, Henry ruled most of France, but he died at an early age.

Henry V was followed by his young son, who, as Henry VI, grew up to be a good man, but a feeble king. The French, led by Joan of Arc, soon won back their country, except the town of Calais.

When Henry VI fell ill, the barons began to quarrel. There were two parties, the House of York and the House of Lancaster, each trying to seize the king's power. As a sign of their party, men wore roses—white for York and red for Lancaster, so these wars between the barons and their followers are called the Wars of the Roses.

The Earl of Warwick, known as Warwick the Kingmaker, was a very powerful baron. Although he won a great victory and made Edward IV king, the wars still went on.

Another important man of this time was William Caxton. When he was a merchant in Flanders, he learned of a new invention—the printing press. In 1476 he set up a printing press of his own in Westminster. This press could print many copies of a book. One of the first books to be printed was Chaucer's *Canterbury Tales*.

Until this time all books were written by hand, by the monks and clerks, so each one took a very long time. A printing press could produce books much more quickly.

Twelve year-old Edward V was murdered in the Tower of London, probably by order of his uncle, who became Richard III.

The long Wars of the Roses ended when Richard was killed in battle, in 1485 and Henry Tudor became king. He was Henry VII, first of the great Tudors. This is the end of the time known as the Middle Ages.

A printing press

Wheþer it be in Batayl subtyltees & remedyes was fynysshed the/Bii ked the/viii/day of June syth I haue okeped

An example of Caxton's printing

A king and his army enter a town

Index

Agincourt   77–78
amusements   25, 54, 63, 64, 65
apprentices   54, 60, 69
armour   8, 11, 14, 61

Bayeux Tapestry   5–7
Becket   27, 38
Black Death   47, 49
Black Prince   44, 49
books   79
Bruce, Robert   44

carts   37, 57
castles   9–12, 14, 26, 43, 46, 57
Caxton   79
Chaucer   38, 79
children   60, 75, 76
clothes   8, 59–62
coaches   37
crime   21, 39, 40, 42
crusades   28, 29

Domesday Book   13

Edward I   43
Edward II   44
Edward III   44, 46
Edward IV   78
Edward V   79

fairs   63
farming   19–24, 47, 74
feudal system   24
food   16, 17, 18, 24, 68, 71, 72, 73
France   44, 45, 77, 78
friars   35
furniture   12, 15, 70

games   25, 46, 54, 65
gilds   53, 64

Harold   5
Hastings   5, 7
Henry I   26
Henry II   27, 40
Henry III   43
Henry IV   49, 77
Henry V   46, 77, 78
Henry VI   78
Henry VII   79
Hereward   26
holidays   25
homage   19
houses   14, 15, 22, 57, 58, 66–71, 74

inns   38

Joan of Arc   78
John   29, 43

lepers   58
Lollards   35, 55
London   50

Magna Carta   29
manors   14, 19, 20, 22, 24, 25, 47
Matilda   26
merchants   37, 55, 57, 60, 69, 70
monasteries   30–34, 57
Montfort, de   43

Normans   5–25, 30, 42
nuns   35

ordeal   39, 40
outlaws   21, 29

pages   18, 44, 75
Parliament   43
Peasants' Revolt   49
pilgrims   27, 36
plays   64
punishments   39–42

Richard I   28
Richard II   49
Richard III   79
roads   37
Robin Hood   29

Saxons   5, 7, 8, 9, 26, 30, 39, 42
schools   33, 76
Scotland   43, 44
shops   51, 52
sport   25, 46, 54, 65
Stephen   26

tapestry   67
tournaments   8, 28, 45, 61
Tower of London   9, 50, 79
towns   50–58
trade   37, 48, 51, 52, 63
travel   29, 36, 37, 38, 57, 63

villeins   19–25, 44, 46, 48, 49

Wales   43
Wars of the Roses   78, 79
weapons   8, 45, 46, 62, 78
William I   5, 8, 9, 13, 14, 26
William Rufus   26
wool trade   47–48
Wycliffe   35